Sizes

Wide and Narrow

Diane Nieker

Heinemann Library
Chicago, Illinois

Customer Service   888-454-2279

Visit our website at www.heinemannraintree.com

Printed and bound in China by South China Printing Company Limited
Photo research by Natalie Gray and Ginny Stroud-Lewis

09 08 07 06 05
10 9 8 7 6 5 4 3 2 1

Library of Congress Cataloging-in-Publication Data

Nieker, Diane.
   Wide and narrow / Diane Nieker.
      p. cm. -- (Sizes)
   Includes bibliographical references and index.
   ISBN 1-4034-7572-5 (lib. bdg.) -- ISBN 1-4034-7577-6 (pbk.)
 1. Size perception--Juvenile literature. 2. Size judgment--Juvenile literature. I. Title.

BF299.S5N543 2005
153.7'52--dc22

                              2005012117

Acknowledgments
Alamy p. **6**; Alamy Images/Robert Harding Picture Library Ltd, Bruno Morandi p. **13**; Corbis pp. **15**(Kevin Fleming), **12**, **16**, **17**; Getty Images/Digital Vision p. **5**; Getty Images/PhotoDisc p. **7**; Harcourt Education/Tudor Photography pp. **4**, **8**, **10**, **18**, **19**, **20**, **21**; Harcourt Education Ltd pp. **9**, **11**; NHPA p. **14**.

Cover photograph reproduced with permission of Getty Images.

Many thanks to the teachers, library media specialists, reading instructors, and educational consultants who have helped develop the Read and Learn/Lee y aprende brand.

Some words are shown in bold, **like this**. They are explained in the glossary on page 23.

Contents

What Does Wide Mean?

Something that has a lot of space from one side to the other is **wide**.

This boy is standing with his feet wide apart.

This lion's mouth is opened wide.

Which Is Wider?

The brown house is wider than the blue house.

The brown house has a wider door.

It has wider windows, too.

Which Is Widest?

This girl is looking for the box with the widest ribbon.

The widest ribbon is wider than any of the others.

Which box should she pick?

The girl picked the box with the widest ribbon.

Did you?

The green ribbon is wider than the blue ribbon.

The red ribbon is the widest of all.

What Does Narrow Mean?

Something that does not take up much space from one side to the other is **narrow**.

These birds are **flamingoes**.

A flamingo's legs
are narrow.

Its neck is narrow, too.

What Other Things Are Narrow?

This plant is called a **spider plant**.

It has a lot of leaves that are very **narrow**.

This sidewalk is very narrow.

There is only room for two people to walk on it.

What Does Narrower Mean?

The trunk of this tree is very wide. If these five children joined hands, they would not reach all the way around.

This tree trunk is much narrower.
One child's arms can go around it.

Which Is Narrowest?

Which line of paint is the narrowest?

The yellow line is narrower than the red line.

But the blue line is narrower than the yellow line.

The blue line is the narrowest.

What Is Width?

When we talk about how **wide** or **narrow** something is, we are talking about width.

You can use a ruler to measure width.

This girl finds the width of the picture.

Quiz: True or False?

1. If something has a lot of space from one side to the other, it is **narrow**.

2. More people can sit on a narrow bench than on a **wide** one.

3. Width means how wide something is.

4. All ribbons are wide.

Glossary

 **flamingo** pink colored bird that has long narrow legs and a long narrow neck

 **narrow** something that does not take up much space from one side to the other

 **spider plant** plant with long narrow leaves

 **wide** something that takes up a lot of space from one side to the other

Index

Answers to quiz on page 22

1. False

2. False

3. True

4. False

Note to parents and teachers

Reading nonfiction texts for information is an important part of a child's literacy development. Readers can be encouraged to ask simple questions and then use the text to find the answers. Most chapters in this book begin with a question. Read the questions together. Look at the pictures. Talk about what the answer might be. Then read the text to find out if your predictions were correct. To develop readers' enquiry skills, encourage them to think of other questions they might ask about the topic. Discuss where you could find the answers. Assist children in using the contents page, picture glossary, and index to practice research skills and new vocabulary.